For Jenny and Karin DC

For Jonathan and Louise JG

First published in Great Britain in 2022
by Scallywag Press Ltd,
10 Sutherland Row, London SW1V 4JT

Text © Deborah Chancellor, 2022
Illustrations © Julia Groves, 2022
The rights of Deborah Chancellor and Julia Groves to be identified
as the author and illustrator of this work
have been asserted by them in accordance with
the Copyright, Designs and Patents Act, 1988

Printed on FSC paper in China by Toppan Leefung

001

British Library Cataloguing in Publication Data available

ISBN 978-1-912650-96-5

MIX
Paper from
responsible sources
FSC
www.fsc.org   FSC® C104723

Deborah Chancellor 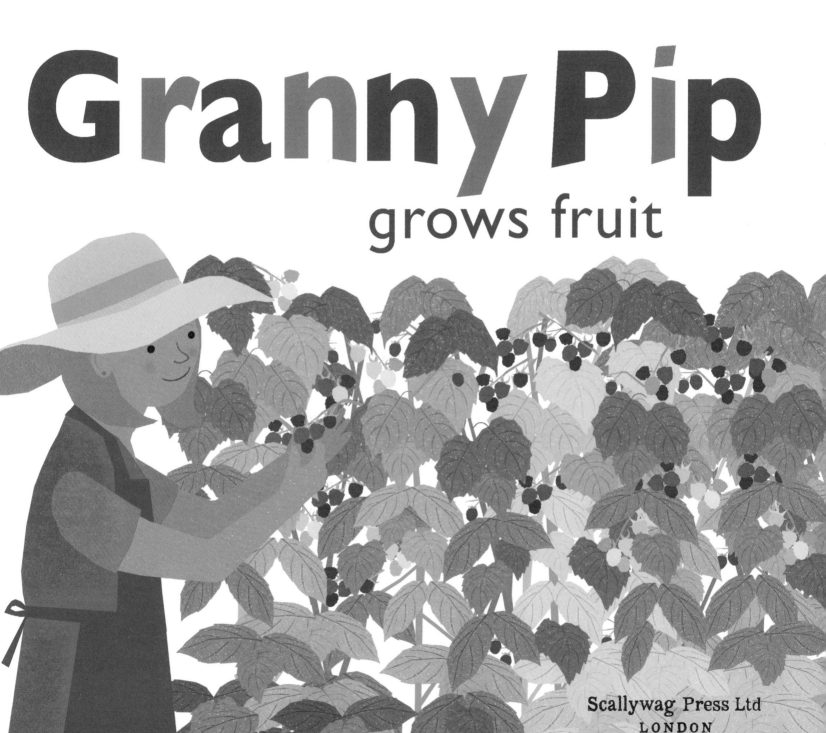 Julia Groves

Granny Pip
grows fruit

Scallywag Press Ltd
LONDON

Granny Pip is busy in her garden.

She works all year to grow fantastic fruit.

Autumn brings strong winds and storms. I help to sweep up piles of fallen leaves,

while Granny spreads the soil
with steamy compost.

Granny digs big holes in the ground for some new raspberry plants. Together we plant a prickly gooseberry bush.

Winter comes with icy frost and snow.

Granny cuts back
tangled apple branches
and prunes her
favourite pear tree.

Spring breezes in with sun and showers.
Granny plants some strawberry seedlings.

We dig up weeds, to give the tiny seedlings space to grow.

The strawberry plants
begin to blossom.

We hang nets over the flowers, to stop birds pecking the fruit that will form.

Summer sunshine dries the earth.

Granny waters . . . and waters . . . and waters . . .
to save her crops from wilting in the heat.

Granny checks her fruit to see if it is ripe.

Her crops are ready to pick at different times.

We mustn't harvest the fruit too soon,
or leave it too late!

The apples and pears are
ripe when summer ends.

I collect all the windfalls
in my basket,
but I can't resist a sweet
and crunchy bite!

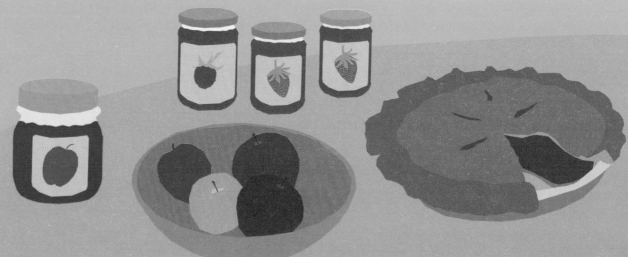

Granny Pip's fruit
is so tasty and fresh.
We eat what we can,
and then cook
or make jam with
the rest.

Follow the trail of pips to match the words and pictures.

Fruit is ripe when it is ready to pick and eat.

A weed is a wild plant that grows where it is not wanted.

When you harvest a crop, you gather it in when it is ripe.

Crops are plants that are grown to be gathered and eaten.

When you prune a plant, you cut off unwanted branches, so it grows better next year.

Compost is natural waste that is used to feed soil and help crops grow.

Plants need water

All plants need food and water to survive. They use water to carry food up to their leaves and back down to their roots. Water is precious, so use it wisely – don't waste tap water on plants. Instead, gather water in a water butt, to sprinkle on your fruit and vegetables when the ground around them is dry.

Close to home

Fruit is grown all over the world. Some of it travels many thousands of miles to end up in your lunchbox! This uses lots of fuel, which is bad for the planet. You can help by eating fruit that was grown closer to where you live. That means only eating local fruit at certain times of the year, when it is ripe and ready to pick.

Sweet Sun

Some kinds of fruit plants love the sun. Their leaves soak up nutrition from the sunshine. The sweeter fruit tastes, the more sun it needs to grow. Strawberries are very sweet, so it's best to plant them in sunny spots. Gooseberries and raspberries have a sharper, tart taste, so they are happy growing in shady places.

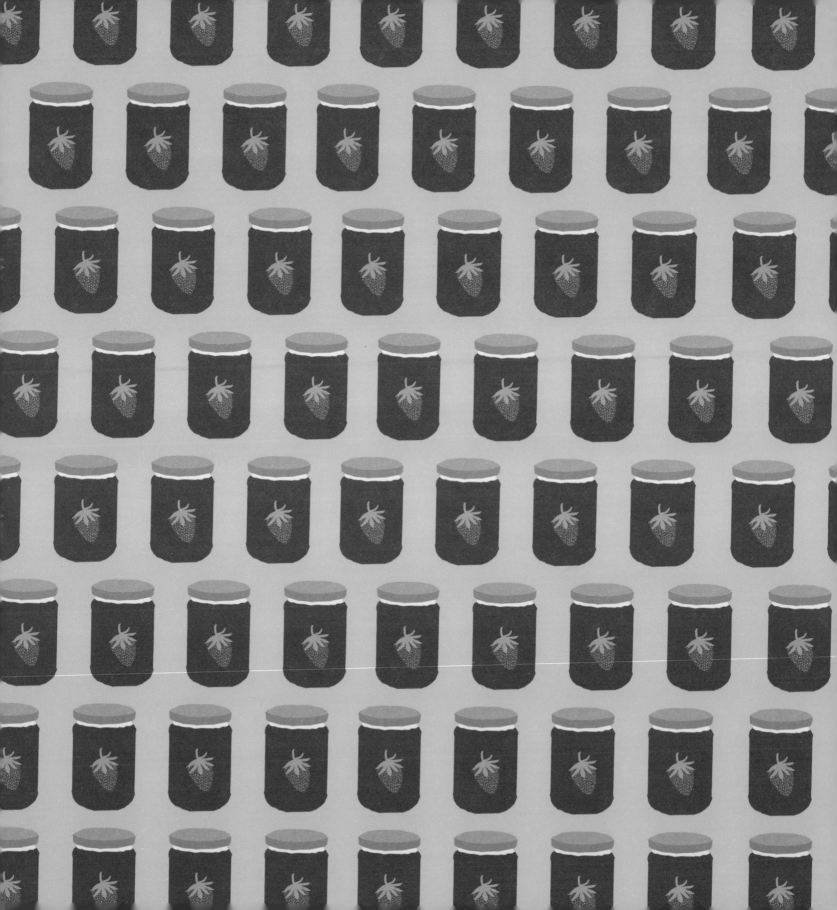